The Beginner's Bible®

Craft and Activity Book

30 Fun Projects Based on Bible Stories

ZONDERkidz

Copyright © 2024 by Zonderkidz

Requests for information should be addressed to:
customercare@harpercollins.com

ISBN 978-0-310-36714-7

Design: Diane Mielke

Printed in the United States

24 25 26 27 28 /CWM/ 7 6 5 4 3 2 1

Welcome!

Inside *The Beginner's Bible Craft and Activity Book* you'll find thirty crafts and activities, from a snake sock puppet and no-sew sheep to a simple bread recipe and scrub-a-dub soap that will keep young hands and minds busy! But that's not all. Each activity has a Bible story reminder and verse to help the children in your life discover God's Word too!

As a parent or teacher, you are an important part of their growth and learning, and will make experiencing these crafts and activities even more fun. Feel free to guide kids through the easy-to-follow instructions and be sure to supervise them when using scissors, a hammer, or while in the kitchen. The items needed to make the crafts will most likely be on hand (you can find a list of the essentials on page 62), but if you're low on supplies or have food allergies, make necessary substitutions. There's no wrong way to do these crafts, and changing things up will allow the child's imagination to shine even brighter. What are you waiting for? Let the fun begin!

Days of Creation

In the beginning, the world was empty. Darkness was everywhere. But God had a plan. He created the world in six days, and on the seventh day he rested.

Have fun moving your body to tell the creation story.

What you need:

- Flashlight
- Bucket or large bowl

What you do:

1. Grab a flashlight. Turn it on. Lift your hand high in the air and say, "On the first day, God created light."

2. Fill a bucket or large bowl with water. Dip your fingers into the bucket and say, "On the second day, God separated the waters and created the sky."

3. Go outside. Jump up and down on a patch of grass. Smell a flower and say, "On the third day, God created dry ground and plants of many shapes and colors."

4. Touch your fingertips together to form a circle. Lift your arms over your head and say, "On the fourth day, God created the sun, moon, and stars."

5. Place one hand directly on top of the other with your palms down. Wiggle your thumbs and say, "On the fifth day, God created swishy fish and flying birds."

6. Swing your arm like an elephant's trunk (or imitate your favorite animal), then place both hands on your hips and say, "On the sixth day, God created animals and the most wonderful creature of all—a person!"

7. Lie down, close your eyes, and say, "On the seventh day, God rested."

In the beginning God created the heavens and the earth.
—Genesis 1:1

Sneaky Snake Sock Puppet

There was a snake in the Garden of Eden. The snake wanted Eve to disobey God. It tricked her into eating the fruit from the forbidden tree. Eve gave some fruit to Adam. He took a bite too.

Create this sneaky snake to remember how important it is to obey God.

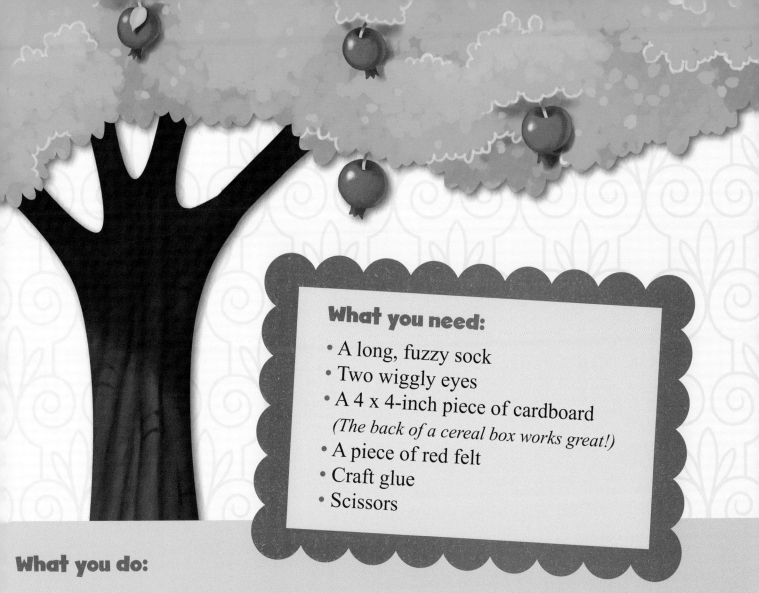

What you need:

- A long, fuzzy sock
- Two wiggly eyes
- A 4 x 4-inch piece of cardboard
  (The back of a cereal box works great!)
- A piece of red felt
- Craft glue
- Scissors

What you do:

1. Turn your sock inside out so the fuzzy side shows.

2. Glue the red felt on the cardboard. Let dry.

3. Fold the piece of cardboard in half so that the felt is on the inside. Holding the folded edge, cut a half circle with scissors to create the mouth. Open it up.

4. Put glue all over the non-felt side of the cardboard, then tuck the mouth inside the toe of the sock.

5. Squeeze a small amount of glue on the back of two wiggly eyes. Place them on the snake.

6. Allow time to dry.

7. Stick your hand inside the sock puppet and tell a friend about the sneaky snake.

Now the serpent was more crafty than any of the wild animals the LORD God had made.

—Genesis 3:1

God's Rainbow Promise

God told Noah to build an ark and take his family and two of every animal on board with him. After everyone was inside, the rain began to fall. And fall.

When the flood finally ended, God put a beautiful rainbow in the sky. It was a sign of his promise to never flood the whole earth again.

Make this rainbow to remember that God keeps his promises!

What you need:

- Colored construction paper *(white, red, orange, yellow, green, blue, and purple)*
- Clear tape or glue stick
- Scissors
- Blue or black marker

What you do:

1. Cut the colored construction paper (red, orange, yellow, green, blue, purple) in half lengthwise, and then into 1-inch strips.

2. Starting with the red strips, create a paper chain by taping or gluing the ends of a strip of construction paper together to form a loop. Insert another strip of paper into the loop. Tape or glue the ends together.

3. Continue adding strips and loops until the paper chain is as long as you want—at least four of each color.

4. Repeat the process with all the other color strips to create a total of six paper chains, one per color.

5. With the marker, draw a large, fluffy white cloud on the white construction paper.

6. Cut out the cloud with your scissors.

7. Tape your paper chains to the backside of the cloud.

8. Display your rainbow for all to see!

[God said,] "I have set my rainbow in the clouds, and it will be the sign of the covenant between me and the earth."
—Genesis 9:13

Blanket Tent

One hot day, Abraham was resting near his tent. Three men came for a visit. They shared exciting news. Abraham's wife Sarah was going to have a baby! Sarah laughed, thinking, *I am too old*. Guess what? The next year, Sarah had a baby boy. They named him Isaac.

Build this tent and remember that anything is possible with the Lord!

What you need:

- Dining room chairs*
- Blankets or sheets
- Heavy books
- Pillows
- Fun things to put inside your tent

What you do:

1. Line up some chairs in a half-circle with the backs of the chairs facing inward.

2. Drape the blankets or sheets over the chairs to make the ceiling and walls of the tent.

3. Place some heavy books on the seats of the chairs so the blankets or sheets don't fall down.

4. Lay a blanket inside the tent and add some comfortable pillows.

5. Fill the tent with anything you'd like: stuffed animals, a flashlight, healthy snacks, and your favorite book of Bible stories. Be sure to welcome anyone who stops by for a visit!

*If you don't have dining room chairs, try spreading a couple of blankets or sheets over a couch, the side of your bed, or a table.

With man this is impossible, but with God all things are possible.
—Matthew 19:26

Colorful T-Shirt

Jacob loved Joseph more than all of his other sons. Jacob made Joseph a colorful robe. Joseph's brothers were jealous. They sold him to some traders. Then they lied to their father and said Joseph had been killed by a wild animal.

Create this colorful T-shirt and remember that God was with Joseph—and God is with you too!

What you need:

- Prewashed, 100-percent cotton, white T-shirt
- Cardboard
- Permanent markers in different colors
- Rubbing alcohol
- Small craft applicator bottle

What you do:

1. Insert the cardboard into the T-shirt to keep the markers from bleeding through to the back of the shirt.

2. With the markers, create a design on your T-shirt. The more colors used, the more vibrant the design. If you add a design on the sleeves, make sure you put a piece of cardboard inside.

3. To give a watercolor effect, use a small applicator bottle and add drops of rubbing alcohol to your design. The more drops used, the bigger the wash effect.

4. Let dry.

5. Remove the cardboard.

6. Before wearing, rinse the T-shirt by hand in cold water. If the colors transfer a bit, don't worry. That adds character to the design!

"Be strong and courageous. Do not be frightened, and do not be dismayed, for the Lord your God is with you wherever you go."
—Joshua 1:9

Pretzel Basket

A new pharaoh ruled over Egypt. He did not like the Israelites. He decided to get rid of all the Israelite baby boys. A woman named Jochebed wanted to save her baby boy. So she gently laid her baby inside a basket and placed him in the river. Pharaoh's daughter saw the basket. She picked up the baby, hugged him, and named him Moses.

Create this fun pretzel basket and remember that God provides!

What you need:

- 1 flat baking pan
- Wooden spoon
- 1 tube cinnamon roll dough
- 350 degree preheated oven
- 1 can frosting
- Pretzels
- 1 can chow mein noodles

What you do:

1. On the flat ungreased baking pan take the cinnamon roll dough and shape it into a ball.

2. With clean hands or wooden spoon, mold the dough to form the basket.

3. Bake at 350 degrees for 10 minutes or until dough is golden brown. Take out and let cool.

4. When the basket is cool, use frosting to line the outside with pretzels and sprinkle chow mein into the basket.

5. Share the story of baby Moses with your family and enjoy this yummy treat!

"And my God will supply every need of yours according to his riches in glory in Christ Jesus."
—Philippians 4:19

Hopping Frog

Pharaoh would not let the Israelites go free. Moses and Aaron told Pharaoh that if he did not let the Israelites leave Egypt, God would punish him. Instead, Pharaoh made the Israelites work even harder. God was not pleased. He sent ten plagues. One of them was frogs! Each time God sent a plague, Pharaoh said he would let God's people go. But then he would change his mind.

Make this hopping frog and remember to listen to God!

What you need:

- 2 paper cups
- Scissors
- Rubber band
- Stapler
- Green and red construction paper
- Glue stick
- Wiggly eyes or white construction paper
- Black marker
- Pencil

What you do:

1. With scissors, make two small snips up the side of a paper cup about ½-1 inch apart. Make the same cuts on the other side of the cup. Fold the slits up to create two tabs.

2. Loop a rubber band around one of the tabs, twist it to form an X across the open end of the cup, then loop the other end around the other tab. Staple both tabs to the outside of the cup to hold the rubber band in place. (You may need a grown-up to help you with this part.) This is the base that makes the frog hop! Set aside.

3. For the frog's body, cut a 4-inch circle out of the green construction paper. Tip: Trace around a small bowl to create the circle.

4. Glue on the wiggly eyes so that half of the eyes hang off the top edge of the paper. (Or use white construction paper and create your own eyes.)

5. With the black marker, draw a mouth and two dots for a nose.

6. For the tongue, cut out a strip of red construction paper. Curl it with a pencil, then glue the tongue on your frog's mouth.

7. For the back legs, fold a piece of construction paper in half. Along the fold, draw a half-circle shape, then add a foot with three toes. Cut around the drawing and open it up. Cut down the middle to create two legs, then use your glue stick to glue the back legs on each side of the circle body.

8. Using the leftover paper from creating the back legs, draw the front legs with a black marker, with two straight lines and three pointy toes per foot. Glue the front legs to the circle body beneath the frog's mouth, so that the feet hang over the bottom edge of the circle. Tip: You can also draw the front legs on the circle body if you are low on construction paper or glue.

9. Once dry, glue your frog to the paper cup base with the rubber band. Let dry.

10. To see your frog hop, place your frog with the rubber band base on top of the other cup, push down to stretch the rubber band, and let go!

"Listen to advice and accept correction. In the end you will be counted among those who are wise."
—Genesis 3:1

Folding Scroll

God led the Israelites to a mountain. Thunder roared and lightning flashed. The people heard a loud trumpet blast. Then God called Moses to the top of the mountain and said, "I am the LORD your God who brought you out of Egypt." God wrote the Ten Commandments on two stone tablets for all his people to obey.

Create this folding scroll to help you learn the Ten Commandments.

1. God is the only true God.

2. Never make idols.

3. Never misuse the Lord's name.

4. Rest on the Sabbath day. Keep it holy.

5. Honor your father and your mother.

6. Do not murder.

7. Husbands and wives must not commit adultery.

8. Do not steal.

9. Do not tell lies.

10. Never want what belongs to others.

What you need:

- Construction paper
- Scissors
- 11 small craft sticks
- Craft glue
- Glue stick
- Markers
- Ribbon or yarn

What you do:

1. Cut out a 9 x 3½-inch piece of construction paper.

2. Glue the craft sticks on the construction paper, leaving space (the width of a craft stick) between each one. Allow time to dry.

3. Flip it over so the paper is on top.

4. Tear out page 63 of this book and cut out the Ten Commandments, or use your favorite Bible translation and write them down on slips of paper yourself for a personal touch.

5. With your glue stick, glue the commandments in order on the sheet of paper, one commandment per craft stick. Let dry.

6. Fold your scroll by going back and forth (accordion-style) with each craft stick.

7. Place a ribbon around your scroll for safekeeping.

"Love the Lord your God with all your heart and with
all your soul and with all your strength."
—Deuteronomy 6:5

Friendship Bracelet

Naomi had a husband and two sons. Ruth was married to one of the sons. Then something sad happened. Naomi's husband and sons died. Naomi told Ruth to return to her parents, but Ruth refused to leave. She loved Naomi so much. Make this friendship bracelet and give it to someone you love.

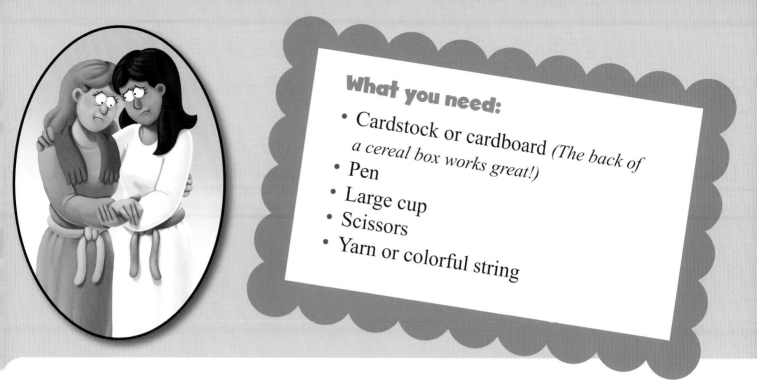

What you do:

1. With your pen, trace around the mouth of the cup on the cardboard to create a circle. Cut it out.

2. Poke a small hole in the center of the circle.

3. Create 8 small, evenly spaced slits around the circle.

4. Cut 7 strands of yarn or colorful string, each the length of your arm.

5. Line up the ends of all 7 strands of yarn and tie a double knot.

6. Push the knot through the center hole of the circle. Keep the knot on the backside while you create your friendship bracelet.

7. Thread each piece of yarn through the slits around the front side of the circle. There will be one empty slit.

8. From the empty slit, count 3 strands to the right. Remove that piece of yarn from that slit and place it in the empty slit. Repeat this step, counting 3 strands to the right of the now-empty slit, then placing that piece of yarn into the empty slit. Do this again and again. The bracelet will naturally form on the backside.

9. When it is long enough to fit around your wrist, remove the bracelet from the cardboard. Tie a knot with the loose ends and trim any excess yarn.

10. Wear your bracelet or give it to a friend!

"One who has unreliable friends soon comes to ruin, but there
is a friend who sticks closer than a brother."
—Proverbs 18:24

Prayer Jar

Hannah wanted to have a baby. She went to the tabernacle and prayed to God. Eli was a priest. He told her God would give her what she asked for. Hannah and her husband had a baby boy! They named him Samuel and thanked God for their new son.

Create this prayer jar and thank God for all he's given you!

What you need:

- Clear jar with lid *(Jelly jars work great!)*
- Acrylic paint in your favorite color
- Puffy paint
- Lace, ribbon, and/or twine
- Small pieces of paper
- Black marker or pen

What you do:

1. Fill the bottom of a glass jar with acrylic paint. Screw the lid on tight. Slowly roll the jar around to get the paint to spread evenly around the inside of the jar. Open the lid and place upside down on a piece of cardboard or paper towel. Allow 24 hours to dry. While drying, shift the jar around occasionally to keep it from sticking.

2. Use puffy paint to create a design on the outside of your jar.

3. Once the paint is dry, add lace, ribbon, or a twine bow around the neck of the jar.

4. Ask a parent to help you write prayer requests on small pieces of paper, such as for family or friends. You can also write down if you are having a hard day or need to forgive someone. Put these requests in your prayer jar. Remember to thank God too!

5. After a few weeks, empty out the prayer jar and see how God has answered your prayers.

Optional: Add stickers, or glue rhinestones or buttons on the outside of your prayer jar to personalize it.

"Devote yourselves to prayer, being watchful and thankful."
—Colossians 4:2

Heart String Art

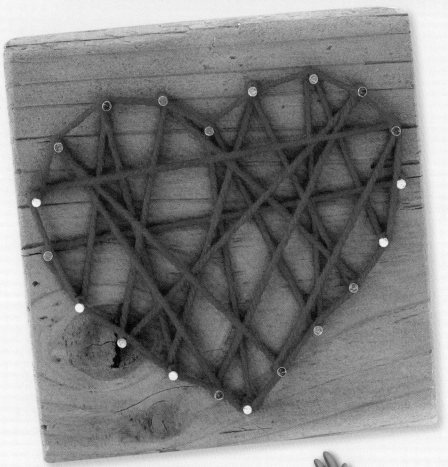

God sent Samuel to find a new king for Israel. Samuel thought Jesse's sons were strong-looking men. But God doesn't look at the outside of a person. He looks at a person's heart. Jesse had another son. David was in the field with the sheep. God told Samuel that David was the next king. Samuel poured oil on David's head, and David was filled with God's power.

Make this string art to remember that God looks at the heart.

What you need:

- 4 x 4-inch *(or larger)* piece of wood
- Piece of paper
- Scissors
- Black marker
- Clear tape
- Small nails *(¾ inch long)* with flat heads
- Small hammer
- Red yarn

What you do:

1. Cut a piece of paper the same size as the wood.

2. Draw a heart on the paper with the black marker. (The heart should almost be as big as the paper.) Make at least 20 evenly spaced dots around the edge of the heart.

3. Tape the drawing to the piece of wood to hold it in place.

4. With an adult's help, poke a nail into one of the dots and tap it in place with the hammer so the nail is halfway in, straight, and no longer wiggly.

5. Continue poking nails into the dots and tapping them in place.

6. Once the nails are sturdy, peel off the paper.

7. Tie one end of the red yarn to one of the nails and double knot it.

8. Start wrapping the yarn around all the nails, creating a unique design.

9. When finished, tie off the yarn on one of the nails.

"The LORD does not look at the things people look at.
People look at the outward appearance, but the LORD looks at the heart."
—1 Samuel 16:7

23

Craft Stick Slingshot

The Philistines were enemies of God and the Israelites. A giant soldier named Goliath wanted to fight the Israelites. King Saul's soldiers were afraid. They did not want to fight the giant. But David wasn't afraid. He said, "God will be with me." David put a stone in his sling and ran toward the giant. He let the stone fly! It hit Goliath's forehead and he fell to the ground dead.

Use this slingshot to remember that God was with David, just like he's always with you!

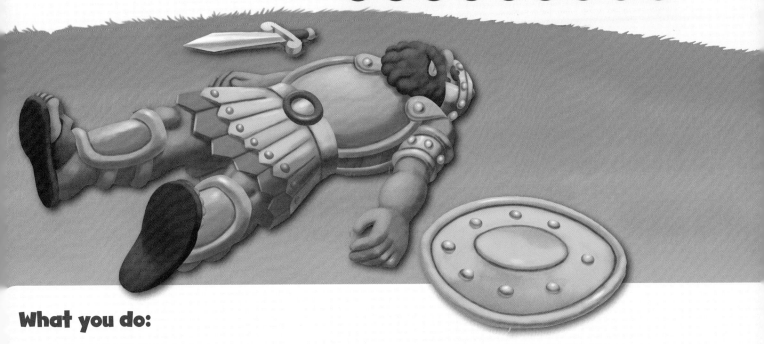

What you do:

1. Place three craft sticks on a paper towel in a Y shape, overlapping the ends. Glue the ends of the sticks together. Allow time to dry.

2. Wrap yarn where the craft sticks meet to reinforce the slingshot.

3. Wrap a rubber band around the top of the Y. Where it touches the craft sticks, place a small amount of glue underneath the rubber band to hold it in place. Let dry.

4. Place a cotton ball in the rubber band and pull back. Let go and watch it fly!

Remember: Do not point the slingshot at animals or people!

*"So do not fear, for I am with you; do not be dismayed, for I am your God.
I will strengthen you and help you; I will uphold you with my righteous right hand."*
—Isaiah 41:10

No-Sew Sheep

King David wrote a song about God. Psalm 23 says the Lord is our shepherd. He gives us everything we need. God gives us strength and comforts us. He guides us down the right paths.

Create this no-sew sheep and remember that the Lord loves his sheep, including you!

What you need:

- White hand towel
- Rubber band
- White, cream, or pink felt
- Scissors
- Craft glue
- Wiggly eyes
- Cotton ball
- Ribbon or yarn

What you do:

1. Open your hand towel and lay it flat.

2. Tightly roll one of the shorter sides of the hand towel to the center.

3. Tightly roll the opposite side to the center.

4. Carefully flip the hand towel over, keeping the rolls in tact.

5. Fold up the bottom, then fold down the top so that the hand towel is folded into thirds and you can see two separate rolls. Hold it together.

6. To create the sheep's legs and feet, wrap a rubber band around a couple of times, 1–2 inches from the bottom edge.

7. For the head, form the sheep's nose by moving the front of the hand towel forward a bit, then taking one part of the rubber band that is around the legs and pulling it over the top.

8. To make the ears, fold the felt in half and cut out a long oval around the fold. Open it up. Push the ears through the layers on the side of your sheep's head until there's one on each side.

9. Glue a pair of wiggly eyes on top along the rubber band and a cotton ball tail in the back. Taking the leftover felt, cut out a triangle nose, and glue it below the eyes.

10. Finish your sheep by wrapping a ribbon around its neck. Give your sheep a hug!

"The LORD is my shepherd, I lack nothing. He makes me lie down in green pastures, he leads me beside quiet waters, he refreshes my soul."
—Psalm 23:1-3

Simple Bread Recipe

God told Elijah to go to a nearby town. There he would find a woman who would take care of him. When Elijah arrived, he saw a poor widow gathering sticks. He asked her for some water and bread. The woman had only a small amount of flour and oil. Elijah told her not to be afraid. The woman made Elijah some bread. Guess what? The woman's flour and oil never ran out after that!

Make this simple bread recipe and remember how God took care of the woman—he will take care of you too!

What you need:

- Large mixing bowl
- Small bowl
- Wooden spoon
- 3-¼ cups all-purpose flour, divided
- 1 packet active dry yeast
- 1 cup warm water
- 1 tbsp clear honey
- 1 teaspoon salt
- ¼ cup butter, melted
- Loaf pan
- Cooking spray
- Clean towel

What you do:

1. Combine 1 cup flour and the active dry yeast in a large mixing bowl.

2. Mix 1 cup warm water and 1 tbsp clear honey into a small bowl. Add to the flour and dry yeast. Stir.

3. Let stand for 10 minutes.

4. Add another cup of flour, 1 tsp salt, and ¼ cup melted butter. Stir.

5. Add 1 more cup of flour and stir.

6. Sprinkle ¼ cup flour on a cutting board or clean surface. Put the dough on top. (It will be very sticky!)

7. Knead the dough with your hands for 10 minutes. To knead, press down with the heel of your hand, then fold the dough in half. Repeat again and again.

8. When the dough is stretchy and not sticky anymore, place the dough in a greased loaf pan.

9. Lay a clean towel over the loaf pan and set it in a warm spot. Allow the dough to rise for 45 minutes.

10. Punch the dough down and let it rise for 10 more minutes. While the dough is rising, preheat the oven to 375 degrees.

11. Bake at 375 degrees for 25 minutes, or until a toothpick comes out clean.

12. Let cool and enjoy!

"Cast all your anxiety on him because he cares for you."
—1 Peter 5:7

Paper Plate Crown

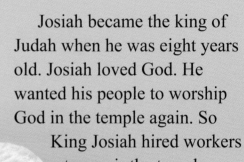

Josiah became the king of Judah when he was eight years old. Josiah loved God. He wanted his people to worship God in the temple again. So King Josiah hired workers to repair the temple.

One day, a priest found a scroll hidden in the wall. When King Josiah read the scroll to the people, they made a promise to obey God's laws.

Create this crown to remind you of King Josiah and how he loved God.

What you need:

- Colorful markers or crayons
- Paper plate
- Scissors
- Craft glue
- Buttons, rhinestones, or small pom-poms

What you do:

1. Color both sides of the paper plate.

2. Fold the paper plate in half.

3. Use your scissors to cut a line up the center of the plate to the ruffled edge. Cut two more lines, one on each side of the center line to create four equal triangles, like a pie. Make sure you leave an inch border all the way around.

4. Unfold the paper plate. Make two more cuts along the folds to the ruffled edge so you now have eight equal triangles.

5. Fold up each triangle to create the crown.

6. Glue buttons, rhinestones, or small pom-poms to the tips of your crown. Let dry. Tip: If you have other art supplies on hand, you could also decorate your crown with stickers, glitter glue, etc. Get creative!

7. Place the crown on your head and pretend you are a king or queen.

"So then, the law is holy, and the commandment is holy, righteous and good."
—Romans 7:12

Fiery Night-light

King Nebuchadnezzar wanted everyone to bow down and worship a golden statue. But Shadrach, Meshach, and Abednego refused. They only worshiped God. The king had the men thrown into a fiery furnace. But when the king looked inside, he saw four men! One of them was an angel from God. Shadrach, Meshach, and Abednego were not hurt. They didn't even smell like smoke!

Make this fiery night-light and remember how God saved Shadrach, Meshach, and Abednego!

What you need:

- Clear plastic cup
- Tissue paper *(orange, red, and yellow)*
- Scissors
- Pencil
- Craft glue
- LED tea light

What you do:

1. Cut the orange, red, and yellow tissue paper into 2 x 2-inch squares.

2. Wrap a square of tissue paper around the eraser end of a pencil. Add a dab of glue on the end and glue the scrunched tissue paper to the outside of the plastic cup.

3. Continue wrapping and gluing until the entire cup is filled with the scrunched tissue paper squares.

4. Allow time to dry.

5. Set your plastic cup on your bedroom nightstand or dresser.

6. Turn on an LED tea light and place it under the cup.

7. Turn off your bedroom light and watch the fire glow, knowing God will keep you safe.

"And everyone who calls on the name of the Lord will be saved."
—Acts 2:21

Paper Plate Lion

King Darius made a new law that everyone must pray only to him. But Daniel kept praying to God, so the king had him thrown into the lions' den. Daniel was not afraid. He knew God would take care of him. The next morning, the king hurried to the lions' den to see if Daniel's God had saved him. Yes! God sent an angel to protect Daniel. King Darius ordered everyone to honor and respect God.

Make this paper plate lion to remember to honor and respect God.

What you need:

- Paper plate
- Yellow crayon
- Orange, yellow, and black construction paper
- Scissors
- Black marker
- Wiggly eyes
- Craft glue
- Pencil

What you do:

1. Color the inside of the paper plate with the yellow crayon.

2. Cut the yellow and orange construction paper in half lengthwise, then into vertical 1-inch strips. Set aside.

3. Cut a small heart from the black construction paper for the lion's nose, then glue it in the center of the paper plate. Tip: If you don't have black construction paper, you can also draw the lion's nose directly on the paper plate using the black marker.

4. Glue on two wiggly eyes above the nose.

5. With the black marker, draw a mouth and whiskers.

6. For the lion's mane, glue the yellow and orange construction paper strips around the outer edge of the plate. Alternate the colors.

7. Add a second row of construction paper strips, framing the center of the plate. Let dry.

8. Curl the tips of each strip by rolling them around a pencil.

Variation: Instead of using wiggly eyes, cut two small holes where the eyes should be and hold it up to your face to create a mask.

"I will praise you, LORD my God, with my whole heart; I will glorify your name forever."
Psalm 86:12

3-D Fish

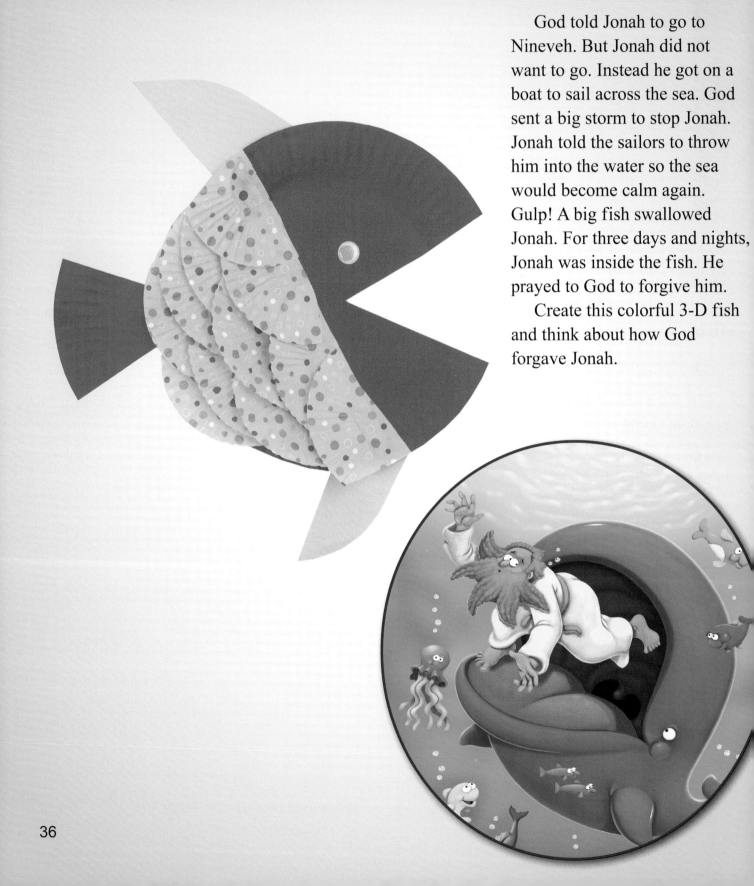

God told Jonah to go to Nineveh. But Jonah did not want to go. Instead he got on a boat to sail across the sea. God sent a big storm to stop Jonah. Jonah told the sailors to throw him into the water so the sea would become calm again. Gulp! A big fish swallowed Jonah. For three days and nights, Jonah was inside the fish. He prayed to God to forgive him.

Create this colorful 3-D fish and think about how God forgave Jonah.

What you need:

- Paper plate
- Paint, markers, or crayons
- Paintbrush *(if using paint)*
- Scissors
- Construction paper *(any color you choose!)*
- Glue stick
- Clear tape
- Wiggly eye
- Colorful paper cupcake liners (6–8)

What you do:

1. Paint or color the inside of a paper plate any color you choose. Let dry.

2. Use your scissors and cut out two fish fins from construction paper. Flip the plate over and glue (or tape) one at the top and one at the bottom of the paper plate fish.

3. On one side of the plate, halfway between the fins, cut a large triangle out of the paper plate for the fish's mouth.

4. For the tail, glue or tape the cut-out triangle to the back of the plate, on the opposite side from the mouth.

5. Glue a wiggly eye above the fish's mouth.

6. Cut cupcake liners in half. Flatten them a bit.

7. Place glue on the straight edge of the cupcake liner and place on the fish in rows, starting at the tail and stopping at the fins, to create 3-D scales.

8. Allow time to dry.

9. Enjoy!

Variation: Use buttons instead of cupcake liners to give the fish a different 3-D effect.

"If we confess our sins, he is faithful and just and will forgive us our sins and purify us from all unrighteousness."
—1 John 1:9

Star Ornament

When Jesus was born, God put a special star in the sky. Some wise men who lived far away saw this star. They knew it was a sign from God that a new king had been born. The star led the wise men to Bethlehem. There they found little Jesus. They worshiped him and gave him gifts fit for a king.

Make this star ornament and remember to worship Jesus.

What you need:

- 8 clothespins
- Craft glue
- Gold paint
- Paintbrush
- Gold glitter
- String or twine
- Scissors

What you do:

1. With an adult's help, carefully take the metal clips off the clothespins.

2. Glue the flat sides of the two wooden prongs of each clothespin together and allow time to dry completely.

3. Lay the wood pieces in the shape of an eight-pointed star and glue together. Let dry overnight.

4. Paint one side of the star gold. Add glitter while the paint is still wet.

5. When the paint is dry, flip the star over and paint and glitter the other side. Let dry.

6. Thread the string through one of the holes in the star and knot the ends together to form a loop. Hang your star ornament on your Christmas tree and sing a Christmas carol to worship Jesus.

"For to us a child is born, to us a son is given, and the government shall be on his shoulders. And he will be called Wonderful Counselor, Mighty God, Everlasting Father, Prince of Peace."
—Isaiah 9:6

Modeling Clay Maze

Every year, Jesus and his family would go to Jerusalem to celebrate the Passover feast. One year on their way home to Nazareth, Mary and Joseph couldn't find Jesus. They went back to Jerusalem and searched for him through the maze of people. Finally, they found him! Jesus was talking with the teachers in the temple. The teachers were amazed that Jesus was very wise for a twelve-year-old boy.

Try this maze and think about how Mary and Joseph searched for Jesus.

What you need:

- Modeling clay
- Box lid *(a shoebox, file box, or pizza box lid works well)*
- Aluminum foil, marble, or extra modeling clay

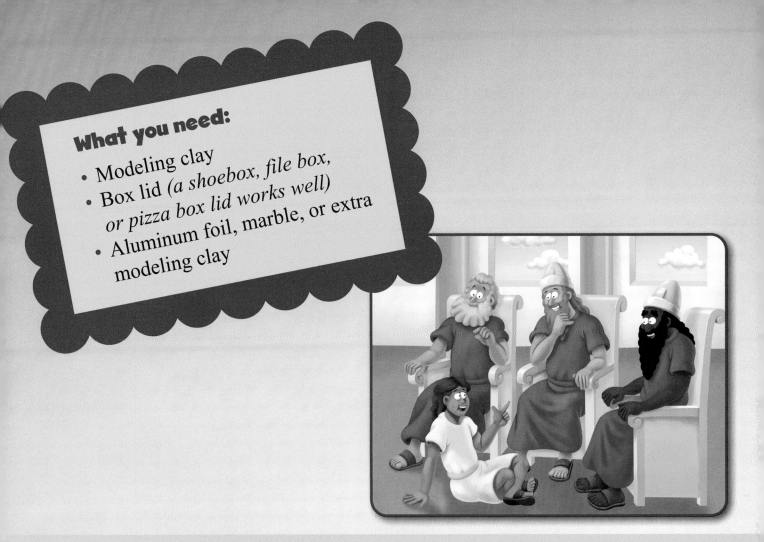

What you do:

1. Roll modeling clay between your hands to create long, worm-like shapes. The more the better!

2. Start your maze by placing one of the worm pieces in the corner of the box lid. Press the clay lightly to stick to the lid.

3. Add more clay worms in different directions to create the maze. Be creative! Curve the clay, keep it straight, even add round bumpers to block the ball if you like. You decide!

4. Once you've completed your maze, make a marble-sized ball by wadding up a piece of aluminum foil. You could also use a marble or extra modeling clay.

5. Place the ball in the starting corner of your maze. Slowly tilt the lid back and forth and watch the ball move through the maze. Make changes to the clay walls if needed.

6. Have a parent, sibling, or friend try out your maze!

"You will seek me and find me when you seek me with all your heart."
—Jeremiah 29:13

Handprint Dove

Many people decided to follow God. John baptized the people in the Jordan River. Jesus asked John to baptize him too. As he did, the Holy Spirit came down from heaven in the form of a dove and landed on Jesus. God said, "This is my Son, and I love him. I am very pleased with him."

Make this dove and think about how much God loves Jesus—and you too!

What you need:

- Paper plate
- Pencil
- Scissors
- Black and yellow markers
- White construction paper
- Clear tape

What you do:

1. Place your hand on a paper plate with your fingertips together touching the ruffled edge and your thumb outstretched.

2. With your free hand, trace your handprint with the pencil.

3. Draw a triangle beak on the side of the thumb outline. Color the beak yellow.

4. Cut out the handprint dove.

5. Draw a black dot above the beak for the eye.

6. Cut a 1-inch horizontal slit in the middle of the handprint where the wings should go. Have an adult help you if needed.

7. For the wings, take the piece of white construction paper and fold the short end down ½–1 inch, creating a flap. Flip the paper over and fold down again, the same width as your flap. Continue flipping and folding accordion-style until the entire paper is folded. (If you pinch one end, it should look like a fan.) Round both of the edges with your scissors.

8. Slide the folded paper into the slit so the wings are the same length. If needed, tape to secure in place. Spread out the wings.

9. Move the dove up and down to watch it "fly."

"I baptize you with water, but he will baptize you with the Holy Spirit."
—Mark 1:8

Disciple Paper Chain

Jesus began telling people about God. He knew he had a lot of work to do, and he went to find some helpers. Jesus found twelve new followers! He called them his disciples.

Make this disciple paper chain and think about how you can follow Jesus and be one of God's helpers too.

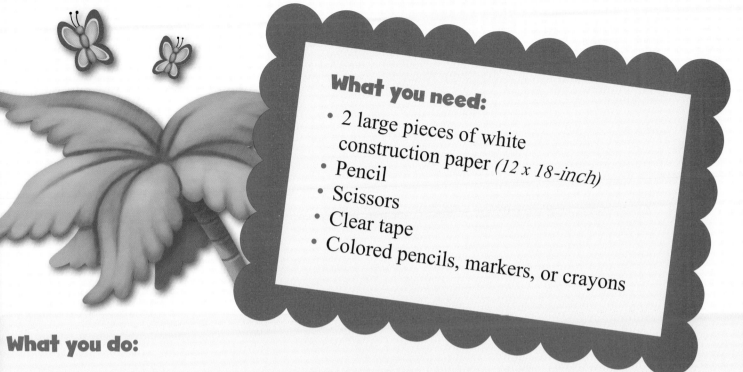

What you need:

- 2 large pieces of white construction paper *(12 x 18-inch)*
- Pencil
- Scissors
- Clear tape
- Colored pencils, markers, or crayons

What you do:

1. Fold a piece of white construction paper in half lengthwise. Open it up and cut along the crease to create two long strips. Repeat this step with the other piece of construction paper.

2. Take one of the strips of paper and fold in half horizontally from left to right, like a book. Fold the top flap and the back flap toward the "spine" to create the letter M. From edge of paper to fold should measure 4.5 inches.

3. Cut out the person template on page 63 and trace it onto the folded paper, or get creative and draw your own outline of a person, using a circle for the head and rectangles for the arms, body, and legs. Whichever method you use, make sure the arms go all the way to the edges of the paper.

4. Cut around the outline.

5. Open it up. You should have a chain of four people!

6. Repeat steps 2–4 with a second strip of construction paper. Tip: You may want to use your first outline as a pattern so that all your disciples are the same size.

7. Repeat steps 2–4 with a third strip. If you mess up any of your three chains, you can use the fourth strip to do it over.

8. When you have all three outlines cut, open your strips and tape your disciple paper chain together. You should now have all twelve disciples.

9. Use your colored pencils and crayons to give the disciples faces and clothes.

Optional: You can also write the names on the back of each disciple.

"Then Jesus said to his disciples, 'Whoever wants to be my disciple must deny themselves and take up their cross and follow me.'"
—Matthew 16:24

Tissue Paper Flower

All sorts of people went to see Jesus. Children, mothers, fathers, grandmas, and grandpas—they all wanted to hear what he was teaching. Jesus told them that God feeds the birds and dresses the flowers in lush leaves and pretty petals. Then Jesus said, "You are much more important than birds and flowers. If God takes care of them, God will take care of you."

Create a tissue paper flower and share it with someone who's important to you.

What you do:

1. Stack the sheets of tissue paper and fold accordion-style (like a fan): Fold the shorter end down ½–1 inch. Flip the paper over and fold down again the same width. Continue flipping and folding until the stack is completely folded.

2. Round the two ends with your scissors.

3. Wrap one end of a chenille stem around the middle of the folded papers. Twist the chenille stem around itself to make it secure.

4. Fan out the tissue paper. Gently pull up one sheet of tissue paper at a time toward the center to create the petals. Do this on both sides.

5. Fluff the flower and give it to a friend!

Variation: Make a whole bouquet of flowers and give it to your mom on her birthday, Mother's Day, or just because!

"See how the flowers of the field grow. They do not labor or spin. Yet I tell you that not even Solomon in all his splendor was dressed like one of these."
—Matthew 6:28–29

Banana Boat Dessert

Jesus and his disciples got into a boat to cross the sea. Jesus took a nap. Suddenly a great storm came up. The disciples were scared. They woke Jesus up. Jesus told the storm to stop. The disciples were amazed.

Have fun making this easy banana boat dessert and think about the amazing things Jesus can do.

What you need:

- Butter knife *(get an adult's help)*
- Plate
- Banana
- Whipped cream, vanilla yogurt, or vanilla ice cream
- Smaller fruit *(such as blueberries, grapes, or strawberries)*
- Granola, nuts, or trail mix

What you do:

1. Peel a banana. Cut it in half and lay it open on a plate so the ends are touching and form an oval.

2. Add a layer of whipped cream, yogurt, or ice cream in the middle.

3. Wash a handful of the small fruit and sprinkle on top.

4. For the final touch, add granola, nuts, or trail mix.

5. Enjoy!

"The men were amazed and asked, 'What kind of man is this? Even the winds and the waves obey him!'"
—Matthew 8:27

Dirty Pig

Jesus told a parable about a man who had two sons. The youngest son didn't want to work anymore. He asked his father for his share of the family money. At first he had fun spending the money, but soon it was all gone. He was so hungry that even pigs' food looked good! The son was sorry for what he had done and went back home. The father was so happy to see his son! God is like that father. He is full of love and joy when people who are lost come back to him.

Create this dirty pig and think about how much God loves you, even when you make mistakes.

What you need:

- Pink construction paper
- Pencil
- Scissors
- 8 x 8-inch baking dish
- Measuring cup
- Plastic spoon
- Brown washable paint
- Liquid dish soap
- Drinking straw
- Black marker
- Sponge *(optional)*

What you do:

1. With your pencil, draw a large circle on the pink construction paper for the pig's head. Add two triangle shapes for ears. For the body, draw a large oval under the head of the pig. Add a curly tail and four long W's for the pig's legs and hooves. (You will draw the face later.)

2. Cut out the pig with your scissors.

3. Fill your baking dish with ½ cup water and four spoonfuls of brown paint. Mix. Next add one squirt of liquid soap. Mix.

4. Blow into your mixture with a straw to create lots of bubbles.

5. Lay your pig facedown into the mound of bubbles. Do this several times and your pig will start to look muddy. Let dry.

6. Once dry, use your black marker to add eyes, an oval snout and nostrils, and a mouth.

Optional: If you'd like your pig to be muddier, put brown paint on the corner of a dampened sponge and pat it directly on the pig.

"God is love. Whoever lives in love lives in God, and God in them."
—1 John 4:16

51

Hosanna Palm Branch

Jesus and his disciples went to Jerusalem for the Passover feast. Jesus rode a donkey into the city. A big crowd welcomed him. People waved palm branches and put them on the road in front of Jesus. They shouted, "Hosanna! Hosanna! Blessed is the king of Israel!"

Create this palm branch and remember Jesus is the true King!

What you need:

- Green construction paper
- Pencil
- Scissors
- Clear tape
- Two large craft sticks
- Craft glue

What you do:

1. With the pencil, outline your hand 6–10 times on green construction paper.

2. Cut out your handprint outlines.

3. Tape your handprints together, starting with one on the top, two below it, and continue working downwards to create a large palm leaf.

4. Glue two craft sticks together to make the handle (stem) thick, and then glue the handle to the bottom of the palm leaf. Allow time to dry.

5. Wave your palm branch and say, "Hosanna! Hosanna! Blessed is the king of Israel!"

"Blessed is he who comes in the name of the LORD! From the house of the LORD we bless you."
—Psalm 118:26

Church Bank

Jesus and his disciples went to the temple area. They watched people drop money into the offering box. The rich people put a lot of money into the box. A poor widow put two small coins into the box. Jesus said, "This woman's gift is greater than all the others. Even though the woman is poor, she gave all the money she had."

Make this church bank and think about how you'd like to give.

What you need:

- Small carton *(milk, whipping cream, etc.)*
- Construction paper *(white and brown or black)*
- Watercolor paint set
- Coffee filter
- Scissors
- Craft glue
- Gold chenille stem

What you do:

1. Wash out the small carton. Let dry.

2. Wrap a piece of white construction paper around the carton, cutting it to fit and gluing it in place. Let dry.

3. Use your watercolor paint set and paint different colors next to each other on the coffee filter. Once dry, cut out "stained glass windows" from the painted coffee filter.

4. Cut out pieces of brown or black construction paper to cover the top of the milk carton for the roof. From the same construction paper, cut out a rectangular door.

5. Glue the roof, windows, and door to the milk carton.

6. Create a small cross with the chenille stem. Glue the cross to the top or side of the milk carton church.

7. To put money into the church bank, open the top like you would to drink milk. Bring your saved money to church on Sunday and give during the offering.

"Each of you should give what you have decided in your heart to give. You shouldn't give if you don't want to. You shouldn't give because you are forced to. God loves a cheerful giver."
—2 Corinthians 9:7 (NIrV)

Scrub-a-Dub Soap

Jesus and his disciples ate a special Passover meal. After supper, Jesus removed his outer clothing. He wrapped a towel around his waist. Then he filled a bowl with water and washed his disciples' feet. By doing this, Jesus showed his friends how to love and serve each other.

Make this fun soap to remind you to love and serve others.

What you need:

- Glycerin soap base cubes *(check your local craft store)*
- Microwave-safe cup
- Spoon
- Food coloring
- Soap scents or essential oils *(optional)*
- Cupcake tray
- Cooking spray
- Small plastic toys or trinkets *(optional)*
- Plastic knife

What you do:

1. Place the glycerin soap base cubes into a microwave-safe cup. Microwave on high for 30 seconds. Stir. Keep microwaving at 30-second intervals until the glycerin soap base cubes are completely melted. (Watch it carefully so that it doesn't boil.)

2. Add a couple drops of food coloring and soap scents or essential oils for color and scent. Stir.

3. Spray the cupcake tray with cooking spray to prevent the soap from sticking. With an adult's help, pour the melted soap into the cupcake tray. (Caution: the glycerin will be hot and can burn.) For fun, add a plastic toy or trinket on top.

4. Put the soap in the refrigerator and chill for 2–3 hours.

5. Use a plastic knife to pop the soap out of the cupcake tray.

6. Take a bath with your new soap … or be like Jesus and wash someone's feet.

**"A new command I give you: Love one another.
As I have loved you, so you must love one another."**
—John 13:34

Stained Glass Cross

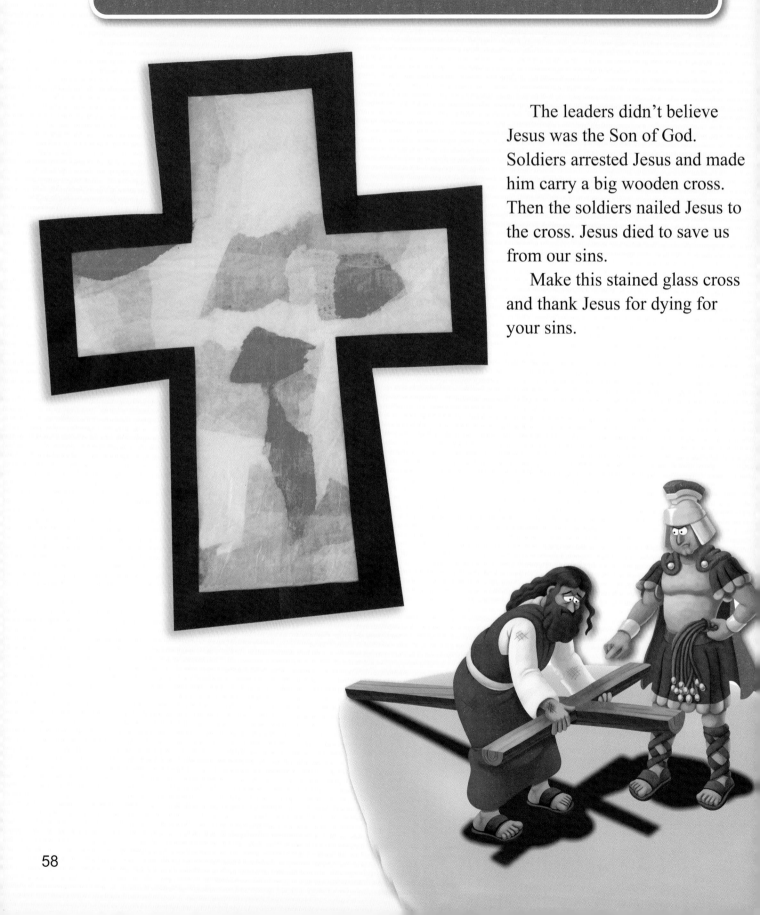

The leaders didn't believe Jesus was the Son of God. Soldiers arrested Jesus and made him carry a big wooden cross. Then the soldiers nailed Jesus to the cross. Jesus died to save us from our sins.

Make this stained glass cross and thank Jesus for dying for your sins.

What you need:

- Tissue paper in different colors
- Wax paper
- Craft glue
- Craft stick
- Construction paper
- Pencil
- Scissors

What you do:

1. Tear the tissue paper into small pieces.

2. Squeeze craft glue all over a 12 x 12-inch piece of wax paper. Spread the glue evenly with a craft stick.

3. Place the tissue paper pieces all over the wax paper so the glue is covered.

4. Squeeze craft glue all over another 12 x 12-inch piece of wax paper. Spread evenly with a craft stick. Place glue-side down onto your tissue paper. Smooth the top with your hand and let dry. Place a large book on top so it dries flat.

5. To make a cross, fold a 9 x 12-inch piece of construction paper in half lengthwise. Draw half a cross along the fold. Cut out the cross and set aside. Open the paper to show the cross-shaped opening.

6. On the back of the construction paper, run a thin line of glue around the cross-shaped opening. Turn the paper over and glue it to the wax paper. Let dry.

7. Once dry, cut around the cross. (optional)

8. Tape your cross to a well-lit window. Beautiful!

Tip: You can decorate your cross cut-out too!

"But here is how God has shown his love for us. While
we were still sinners, Christ died for us."
—John 13:34

Coffee Filter Angel

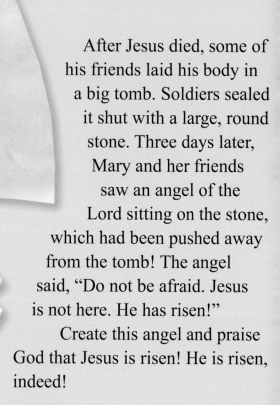

After Jesus died, some of his friends laid his body in a big tomb. Soldiers sealed it shut with a large, round stone. Three days later, Mary and her friends saw an angel of the Lord sitting on the stone, which had been pushed away from the tomb! The angel said, "Do not be afraid. Jesus is not here. He has risen!"

Create this angel and praise God that Jesus is risen! He is risen, indeed!

What you need:

- 2 coffee filters
- Scissors
- Puffy paint in gold or silver *(optional)*
- Craft glue
- White cotton ball, or construction paper and markers
- Craft stick
- Gold or silver chenille stem
- Clear tape

What you do:

1. Fold a coffee filter in half, and then fold in half again. Cut along the creases to create two wings.

2. Flatten the other coffee filter. Fold in half. Fold in half again or tuck the sides in a bit to create the size robe you want.

3. Glue a cotton ball to the craft stick for the head, or if you'd like to draw a face on your angel, cut a circle from construction paper and draw a face with markers before gluing it to the craft stick. Let dry.

4. Snip the top of the angel's robe. Add a dot of glue to the back of the craft stick right below the head and place the craft stick inside the slit of the angel's robe, pressing the robe against the stick to secure it.

5. To attach the wings, add a drop of glue to the back of the robe underneath the head. Let dry.

6. Create a small circle halo with the chenille stem. Cut the chenille stem, leaving enough length to tape the halo to the back of the angel.

7. Display the angel to remind yourself that Jesus is risen!

(Optional: For added decoration, use gold or silver puffy paint to decorate the skirt of your angel. Let dry.)

Essential Supplies

These supplies can be used to make many of the crafts in this book, so it's a great idea to have them on hand!

Scissors

Craft glue

Construction paper

Markers

Cardboard

Pen and/or pencil

Wiggly eyes

Craft sticks

Paintbrushes

Ribbon, yarn, and/or string

Rubber bands

Cotton balls

Coffee filters

Paper plates

Tissue paper

Felt fabric

Paper towels

Wax paper

Crayons or colored pencils

Paint (puffy, acrylic, and watercolor)

Clear tape and/or glue stick

Clear plastic and paper cups

Chenille stems

Wooden and plastic spoons

Small, medium, and large bowls

Craft Templates

Cut out Ten Commandments for "Folding Scroll" craft.

1. God is the only true God.

2. Never make idols.

3. Never misuse the Lord's name.

4. Rest on the Sabbath day. Keep it holy.

5. Honor your father and your mother.

6. Do not murder.

7. Husbands and wives must not commit adultery.

8. Do not steal.

9. Do not tell lies.

10. Never want what belongs to others.

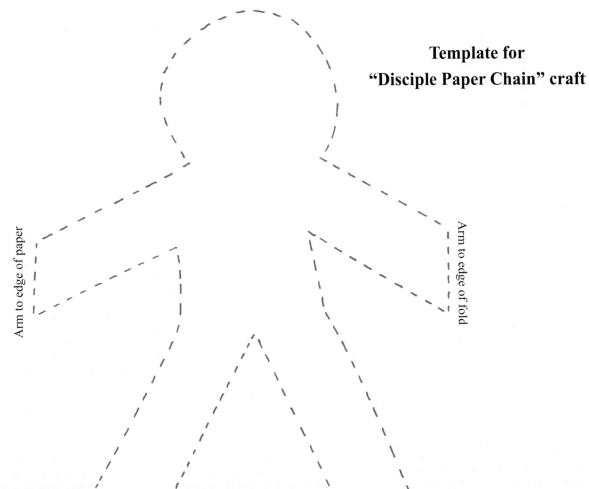

Template for "Disciple Paper Chain" craft

Arm to edge of paper

Arm to edge of fold